Little Scientists, BIG Questions

I0794759

What Does an Engineer Do?

Written by Ruth Owen and Designed by Alix Wood

WINDMILL BOOKS

Published in 2025 by Windmill Books,
an Imprint of Rosen Publishing
2544 Clinton St.
Buffalo, NY 14224

Cataloging-in-Publication Data

Names: Owen, Ruth.
Title: What does an engineer do? / Ruth Owen.
Description: Buffalo, New York : Windmill Books, 2025. | Series: Little scientists, big questions
Identifiers: ISBN 9781538395394 (pbk.) | ISBN 9781538395400 (library bound) | ISBN 9781538395417 (ebook)
Subjects: LCSH: Engineers--Juvenile literature. | Engineering--Juvenile literature.
Classification: LCC TA157.O94 2025 | DDC 620--dc23

Image Credits:
Alamy: 7 (David Parker); Creative Commons: 16; NASA: 9, 10, 12, 13B; Science Photo Library: 14 (Nano Calvo, VW Pics); Shutterstock: Cover (UNIKYLUCKK), 4 (Yeti Studio/Kaspars Grinvalds/Hong Vo/Wuttichok Panichiwarapun/Laura Stubbs/goir/Natdanai99/Gianluca Cinnante), 5 (nblx), 6T (Sandra Polo), 6B (Juice Flair), 8 (Andrey Yurlov), 11 (freestyle images), 13T (Storyet), 15 (SkyPics Studio), 17 (Reshetnikov Art), 18T (engel.ac), 18B (goodluz),19 (Jacques Tarnero), 20 (Elena Noeva/Jacob Lund), 21 (Elena Noeva), 22T (Andrey Popov), 22B (WinWin Artlab), 23 (Costazzurra); Alix Wood/Ruby Tuesday Books: 2–3.

Printed in the United States of America

CPSIA Compliance Information: Batch #CSWM25
For Further Information contact Rosen Publishing at 1-800-237-9932

What is an engineer?

Great guessing, little scientists.
An engineer does all those things!

Engineers invent, design, and build the things that people use every day.

The things engineers build solve problems in our world.

To do their work, engineers use lots of **science**.

An engineer designed this bridge.

There are lots of different types of engineers.

Some engineers design and build skyscrapers, roads, and bridges.

Some engineers build engines and other machines.

Robot and computer engineers design and build robots.

These robots work in a big building called a warehouse.

Each robot has a computer inside!

The robots are carrying books, games, and other things for sale.

People buy these things online.

Get ready for some BIG science!

To invent something new, an engineer works step by step.

Let's work with a space robot engineer!

STEP 1 : What is the problem?

How can we explore the surface of Mars?

This means the engineer must find out lots of facts about Mars.

They use space science, robot spacecraft, and computers.

This robot spacecraft flies around Mars and sends information back to Earth.

It is freezing cold on Mars.

Mars has almost no air.

Mars is millions of miles from Earth.

STEP 3 :
Design something that solves the problem.

A robot rover could go to Mars and explore the planet's surface.

A robot doesn't need air or water. It won't care that it's dangerous on Mars.

Engineers draw their designs on paper.

Mars robot rover idea

Sometimes they design them on a computer.

STEP 4 :
Build a prototype.

Next, an engineer uses science and tools to build a prototype, or model, of their idea.

They use the model to test if their design will work.

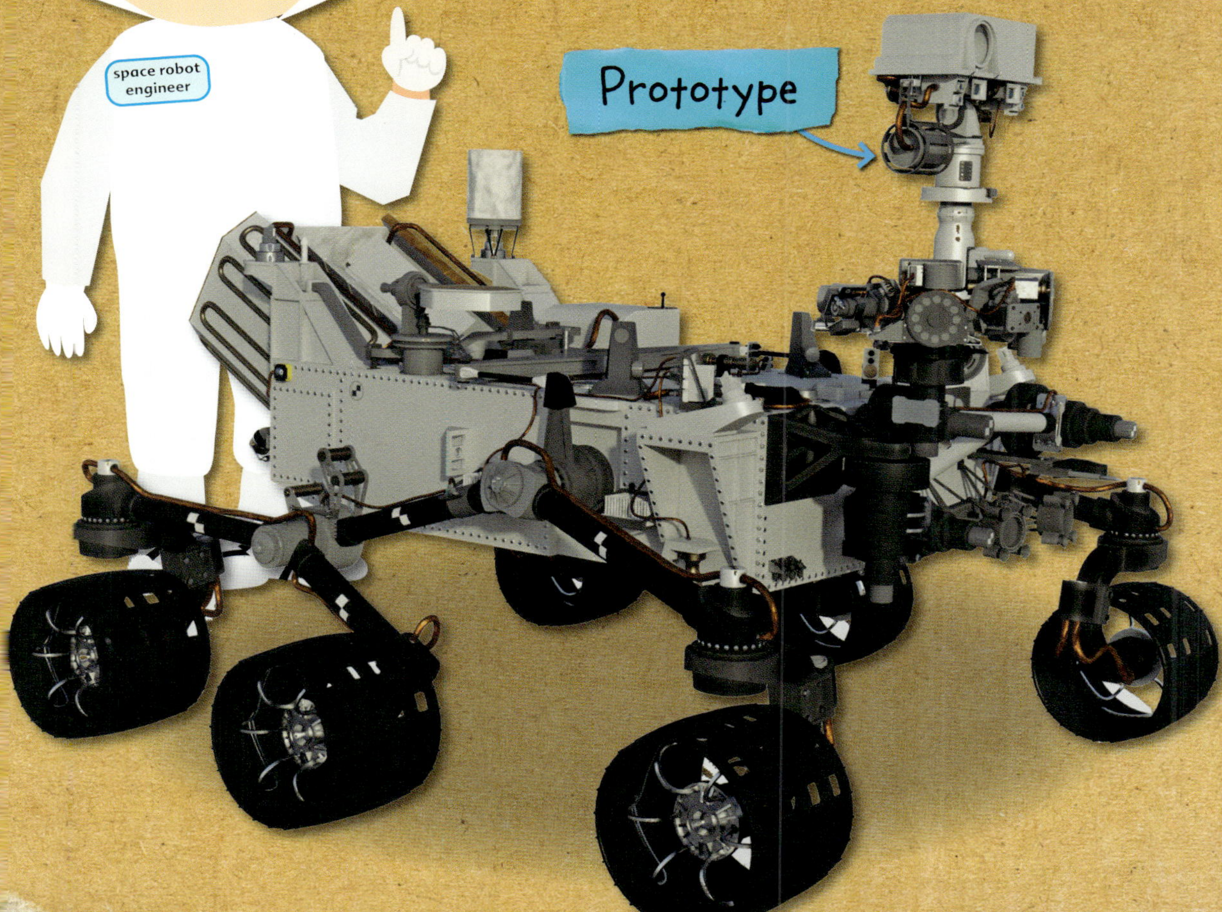

STEP 5 :
Test, test, and test again!

Once an engineer builds their idea, they test it again and again.

These engineers are testing if the robot can drive over bumpy ground on Mars.

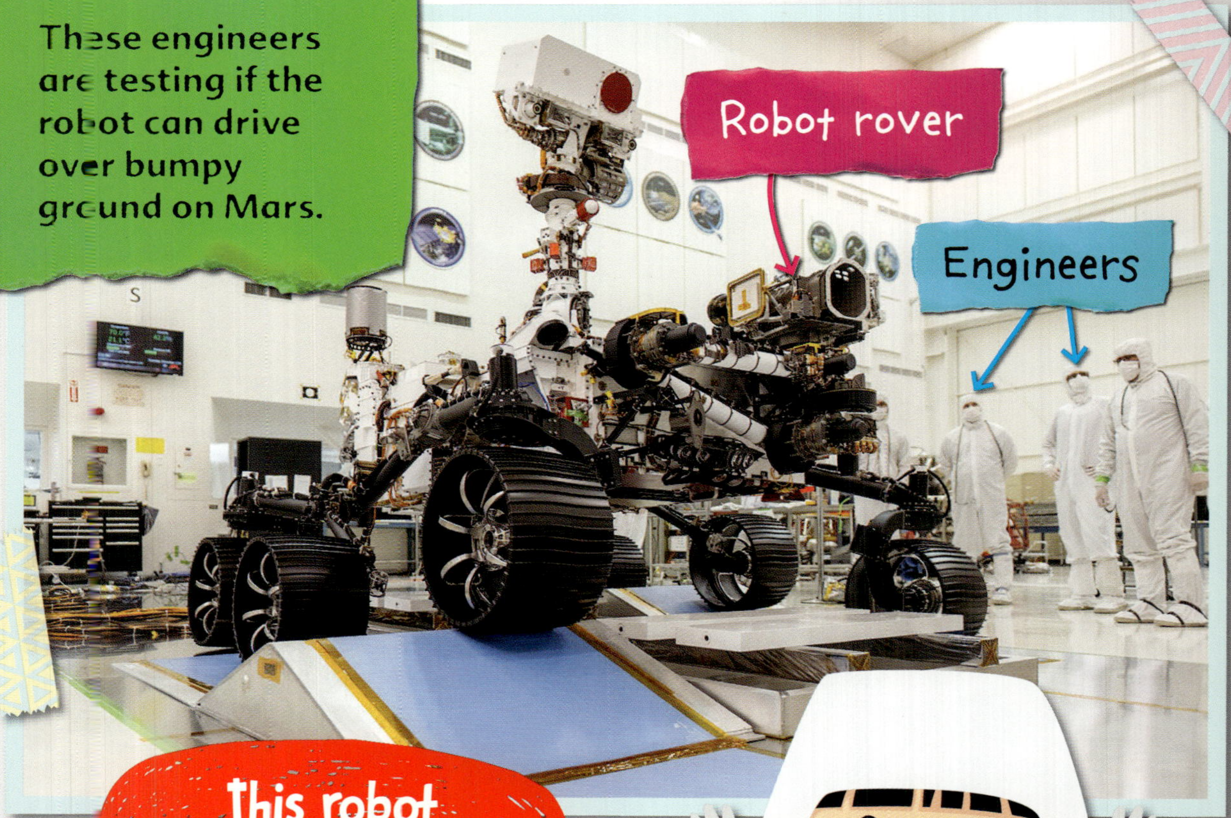

STEP 6 :
Try again!

Sometimes an idea doesn't work and an engineer must try again.

But don't worry! This can make the idea better next time.

Oh dear! Our robot needs more work.

This is a robot called *Perseverance*. It is exploring Mars.

Engineers invented a machine called a 3D printer.

It makes a solid, plastic object from a picture on a computer.

Engineers use 3D printing to make prototype models.

Get ready for some BIG science!

How does a 3D printer work?

1: The engineer draws an object on a computer.

2: The printer copies the drawing.

3: The printer makes the object from thin layers of hot, liquid plastic.

4: The plastic cools and becomes solid.

Some engineers wanted to help children with limb differences.

A child may be missing a part of their arm because they had an accident.

Some children are born with limb differences.

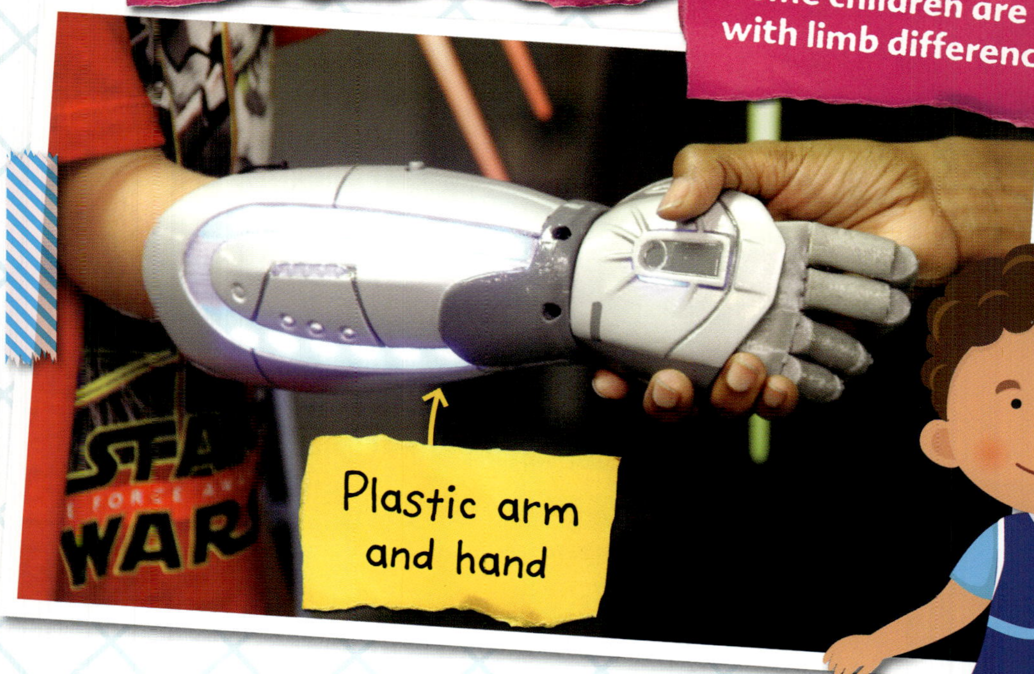

The engineers invented plastic arms and hands that children can wear and use.

The arms and hands are called prosthetic limbs. The engineers used lots of science facts about the human body to think up their designs.

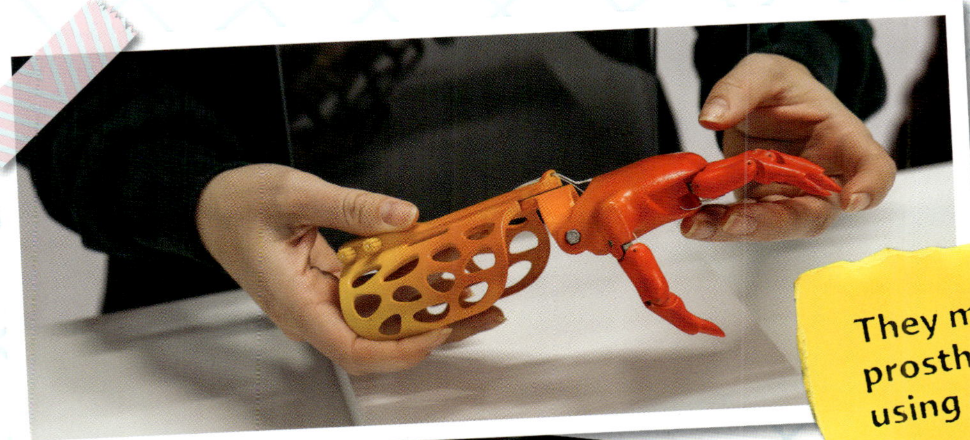

They make the prosthetic limbs using a 3D printer.

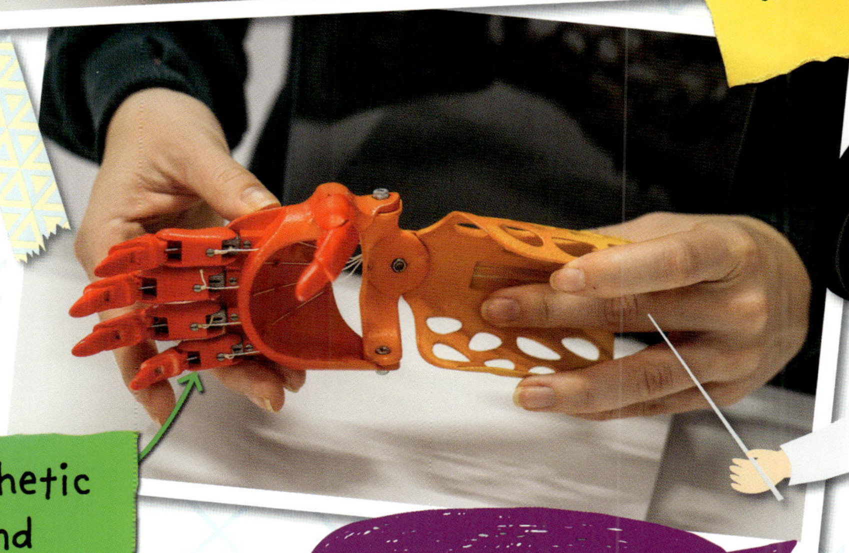

Some engineers design things to help our planet.

They design and build wind turbines that make eco-friendly electricity.

The blades of a wind turbine turn a machine that makes the electricity.

A wind turbine engineer must know the science of how wind blows.

Then they can design blades that catch lots of wind to make lots of electricity.

A roller coaster engineer must know all about forces and energy.

Then a force called gravity pulls the cars down!

As the cars whiz down the big hill, they pick up speed.

The energy pushes the cars around the rest of the ride.

Engineers use science to design a fast and exciting ride.

Some engineers know all about electricity and machines.

They design and build machines we use in our homes.

What will engineers design and build in the future?

Now we know how engineers use science.
Good work, little scientists!

My Science Words

eco-friendly
Something that is good for our planet and doesn't cause damage or pollution.

gravity
The force that pulls everything on Earth down towards the ground.

invent
To think up and create something new.

prototype
A model or first version of something new that can be used for testing.